PHYLLIS J. LE PEAU &

CARING
—*FOR*—
SPIRITUAL
NEEDS

*9 Studies for Groups
or Individuals*
With Notes for Leaders

CARING PEOPLE BIBLE STUDIES

INTERVARSITY PRESS
DOWNERS GROVE, ILLINOIS, USA
LEICESTER, ENGLAND

InterVarsity Press, USA, is the book-publishing division of InterVarsity Christian Fellowship, a student movement active on campus at hundreds of universities, colleges and schools of nursing in the United States of America, and a member movement of the International Fellowship of Evangelical Students. For information about local and regional activities, write Public Relations Dept., InterVarsity Christian Fellowship, 6400 Schroeder Rd., P.O. Box 7895, Madison, WI 53707-7895.

Inter-Varsity Press, UK, is the book-publishing division of the Universities and Colleges Christian Fellowship (formerly the Inter-Varsity Fellowship), a student movement linking Christian Unions in universities and colleges throughout the United Kingdom and the Republic of Ireland, and a member movement of the International Fellowship of Evangelical Students. For information about local and national activities write to UCCF, 38 De Montfort Street, Leicester LE1 7GP.

All Scripture quotations, unless otherwise indicated, are from the Holy Bible, New International Version. Copyright ©1973, 1978, International Bible Society. Used by permission of Zondervan Bible Publishers. Published in Great Britain by Hodder and Stoughton Ltd.

Some of the studies in this guide are adapted from studies written by Nurses Christian Fellowship staff.

Study 7 is adapted from Andrew T. & Phyllis J. Le Peau, James: Faith That Works (Downers Grove, Ill.: InterVarsity Press, 1987), pp. 14-17, 52-53.

Cover photograph: Michael Goss

USA ISBN 0-8308-1194-X
UK ISBN 0-85111-333-8

Printed in the United States of America

15	14	13	12	11	10	9	8	7	6	5	4	3	2	1
03	02	01	00	99	98	97	96	95	94	93	92	91		

Getting the Most from Caring People Bible Studies

Caring People Bible Studies are designed to show how God equips us to help others who are in need. They reveal what the Bible has to say about the pain we will all face in life and what we can do to care for friends, family, neighbors and even strangers who experience pain.

The passages you will study will be thought-provoking, challenging, inspiring and practical. They will show you how to focus on others, but they will also help you focus on yourself. Why? Because these guides are not designed merely to convince you of the truthfulness of some idea. Rather, they are intended to allow biblical truths to renew your heart and mind.

These Bible studies are inductive rather than deductive. In other words, the author will lead us to discover what the Bible says about a particular topic through a series of questions rather than simply telling us what she believes. Therefore, the studies are thought-provoking. They help us to think about the meaning of the passage so that we can truly understand what the biblical writer intended to say.

Additionally, these studies are personal. At the end of each study, you'll be given an opportunity to make a commitment to respond. And you will find guidance for prayer as well. Finally, these studies are versatile. They are designed for student, professional, neighborhood and/or church groups. They are also effective for individual study.

How They're Put Together

Caring People Bible Studies have a distinctive format. Each study takes about forty-five minutes in a group setting or thirty minutes in personal study—unless you choose to take more time. The guides have a workbook format with space for writing responses to each question. This is ideal for personal study and allows group members to prepare in advance for the discussion. At the end of the guides are some notes for leaders. They describe how to lead a group discussion, give helpful tips on group dynamics, suggest ways to deal with problems which may arise during the discussion, and provide additional background information on certain questions. With such helps, someone with little or no experience can lead an effective study.

Suggestions for Individual Study

1. As you begin the study, pray that God will help you understand and apply the passages to your life. Pray that he will show you what kinds of action he would have you take as a result of your time of study.

2. In your first session take time to read the introduction to the entire study. This will orient you to the subject at hand and the author's goals for the studies.

3. Read the short introduction to the study.

4. Read and reread the suggested Bible passage to familiarize yourself with it.

5. A good modern translation of the Bible, rather than the King James Version or a paraphrase, will give you the most help. The New International Version, the New American Standard Bible and the Revised Standard Version are all recommended. However, the questions in this guide are based on the New International Version.

6. Use the space provided to respond to the questions. This will help you express your understanding of the passage clearly.

7. It might be good to have a Bible dictionary handy. Use it to look up any unfamiliar words, names or places.

8. Take time with the final question in each study to commit yourself to action and/or a change in attitude.

Suggestions for Group Study

1. Come to the study prepared. Follow the suggestions for individual study mentioned above. You will find that careful preparation will greatly enrich your time spent in group discussion.

2. Be willing to participate in the discussion. The leader of your group will not be lecturing. Instead, he or she will be encouraging the members of the group to discuss what they have learned. The leader will be asking the questions that are found in this guide.

3. Stick to the topic being discussed. Your answers should be based on the verses which are the focus of the discussion and not on outside authorities such as commentaries or speakers.

4. Be sensitive to the other members of the group. Listen attentively when they describe what they have learned. You may be surprised by their insights! When possible, link what you say to the comments of others. Also, be affirming whenever you can. This will encourage some of the more hesitant members of the group to participate.

5. Be careful not to dominate the discussion. We are sometimes so eager to express our thoughts that we leave too little opportunity for others to respond. By all means participate! But allow others to also.

6. Expect God to teach you through the passage being discussed and through the other members of the group. Pray that you will have an enjoyable and profitable time together, but also that as a result of the study, you will find ways that you can take action individually and/or as a group.

7. We recommend that groups follow a few basic guidelines, and that these guidelines be read at the beginning of the first session. The guidelines, which you may wish to adapt to your situation, are:

☐ Anything said in the group is considered confidential and will not be discussed outside the group unless specific permission is given to do so.

☐ We will provide time for each person present to talk if he or she feels comfortable doing so.

☐ We will talk about ourselves and our own situations, avoiding conversation about other people.

☐ We will listen attentively to each other.

☐ We will be very cautious about giving advice.

☐ We will pray for each other.

8. If you are the group leader, you will find additional suggestions at the back of the guide.

Introducing Caring for Spiritual Needs

I met Anne at the hospital where I was working. She was in an isolation room because she had hepatitis caused by using contaminated needles. She had been on drugs. As often as possible, I spent extra time with her. In a short time I found out that she had an alcoholic father whom she hated, that her parents were divorced and her mother was remarried, and that she had experienced sexual relationships with several young men. In the midst of great physical and emotional needs, her spiritual needs also became evident.

Because Anne had never known the love of an earthly father, God's love seemed foreign to her. Yet she needed to be loved. Anne had never experienced being forgiven, but she felt guilt. Some of her emotional and physical symptoms seemed to stem from a lack of meaning and purpose in her life. We spoke often of God's love. Sometimes she was quite responsive. At other times she was defensive and reactive. Eventually, Anne came to know Jesus. The deep need for her spirit to be in a right relationship with God was met.

And her life changed. Anne got off drugs. She became involved with a group of Christians. She prayed. She worked at healing her relationship with her parents. Later she married and established a Christian home. Her life was not perfect. There were still scars—but it was better.

Everyone has spiritual needs—both the helper and the helped, and both Christians and non-Christians. We need help to establish and maintain a dynamic relationship with God. Seldom is there an obvious set of symptoms of spiritual need. If we want to help meet spiritual needs we must develop a sensitive ear and a willingness to respond to tiny clues.

People are integrated beings created to live in harmony with God, ourselves and other people. To maintain harmonious relationships, we must first establish right relationships. I believe that a person who wants a harmonious relationship with himself or herself and rich meaningful relationships with other people must first establish and work at a right relationship with God. God is the key to physical, emotional, social and spiritual integration.

Therefore a spiritual need is, by definition, the lack of any factor or factors necessary to establish and maintain a dynamic, personal relationship with God.

Because we live in a culture in which the material—what we see, touch, feel, smell—has been made all-important, we often ignore the spiritual. The purpose of this guide is to help make us more aware of spiritual needs, both in ourselves and in others. It should also help us to meet those needs.

It is not possible to create a guide covering every spiritual need. Neither is it possible to clearly differentiate between the spiritual and the emotional. The need to be loved, for example, is an emotional as well as a spiritual need. We are integrated. We need to be loved by God; we need to be loved by each other. If we know God's love, that love can help us to love and be loved by others. The physical is involved too. The body can deteriorate if we are not loved. In spite of these blurred causes and effects, it is possible to look at symptoms, gather information from the person, and determine ways to help someone in spiritual need.

This guide is for people who want to grow in caring for those who are in spiritual need. The first two studies, "What Are Spiritual Needs?" and "Recognizing a Spiritual Need," will help you increase your ability to recognize spiritual needs. The other studies look at specific spiritual needs, such as the need for a relationship with God, for meaning and purpose, for belonging and love, and for persevering in faith.

May your own relationship with God deepen as you seek to care for others who are in spiritual need.

1/What Are Spiritual Needs?
Psalm 38

I was in deep spiritual need and did not know it. I was a Christian, after all, and had attempted almost all my life to walk closely with God. But I allowed myself to become self-sufficient. I lived life *my way* rather than God's. All of my person was affected. If I had written a description of myself at that time, it could have sounded much like this psalm.

1. When are you most likely to be aware of your spiritual needs?

2. Read Psalm 38. What clues to David's spiritual needs do you find in this psalm?

3. What physical symptoms did he exhibit?

4. What emotional responses accompanied his illness?

5. How did the psalmist perceive his friends and family (vv. 11-22)?

his enemies?

6. Describe a time when your sin or distance from God has created a comparable situation for you.

What was helpful to you at that time?

7. If you had been a friend of David's, what might you have done to meet his physical, emotional and spiritual needs? (Be specific.)

8. How did the psalmist respond to his own needs (vv. 15-18, 21-22)?

9. What is involved in "waiting" for the Lord for yourself or for another in deep pain?

10. What role does confession play in your relationship with God and your total well-being?

11. What are your spiritual needs right now?

How could they be met?

Express your spiritual needs to God. Ask him to meet those needs.

2/Recognizing Spiritual Needs
Matthew 9:1-13

I t was difficult to care for Jeanne. To be quite frank, many nurses did not go into her room because of her unreasonable demands. One day after making her comfortable I took her hand. Her voice was anxious. She said, "Please don't ever leave me!"

I responded, "Jeanne, I will have to leave you. But I know someone who loves you very much and will never leave you." That day her deepest need, a spiritual need, began to be met by the one who came to call sinners to repentance.

1. Think about a time that you recognized a spiritual need in someone. How did you know that it was a spiritual need?

2. Read Matthew 9:1-8. What do you think the paralytic and his friends were expecting from Jesus?

3. Why do you think Jesus offered the paralytic forgiveness?

4. What role did the man's friends play in this process?

5. How does your faith in Jesus affect what you do for those who are in spiritual need?

6. What do you think accounts for the difference in the response of the teachers of the Law and the response of the crowd to Jesus?

7. Read Matthew 9:9-13. How was Christ's calling of Matthew similar to his healing of the paralytic?

8. Compare the Pharisees' response to Jesus in this episode to that of the teachers of the Law in the first episode. What do you think was the basic concern of both?

9. How did Christ's response to the teachers of the Law and the Pharisees demonstrate his recognition of their spiritual needs?

---

10. Who are the people mentioned in verse 12? (Consider the "healthy," the "sick," the "physician.")

---

11. How did Jesus "show mercy"?

---

12. What have you learned from this passage that will help you recognize and respond to the spiritual needs of others?

Pray that God will help you to become aware of and sensitive to the spiritual needs of others.

3/The Need for a Relationship with God
Romans 5:1-11

J o Ann thought *that she came to our house that day to talk about her up-coming surgery.* She really came because she needed to know God. I listened closely to her words. Then I asked questions like "What is it that you are afraid of?" "When you think about God, what do you feel and what do you think about?" and "How meaningful is prayer to you?" It became apparent, not only to me, but to Jo Ann that her natural apprehension about surgery had triggered awareness of a more central need. Jo Ann was seeking a relationship with God.

---

1. Under what kinds of circumstances do you feel best about your relationship with God?

---

2. Read Romans 5:1-11. According to this passage, what are the benefits of a right relationship with God?

3. What is it like for you to be at "peace" with someone after hostility and conflict?

4. What does it mean that we "have gained access by faith into this grace in which we now stand" (v. 2)?

How does this work of God's grace continue in your life today?

5. In verses 2-5 what is the connection between rejoicing "in the hope of the glory of God" and rejoicing "in our sufferings"?

6. What difference does it make in our relationship with God that he loved us even before we turned to him (v. 8)?

7. What all did God make possible for us through Christ's death and Christ's life (vv. 9-10)?

8. In what ways do you see faith, hope and love as ingredients in our relationship with God (vv. 1-8)?

_____

9. What difference could it make to someone who is in spiritual need if you could offer faith, hope and love to that person?

_____

10. In summary, what do you have to offer from this passage to someone who has the spiritual need of a right relationship with God?

_____

Ask God to show you how you need to make your relationship right with him today.

4/The Need for Meaning and Purpose
1 Peter 1:1-16, 22-25

I t is impossible to describe the despair that I have seen in someone who has lost a sense of meaning and purpose to life.

In his *Man's Search for Meaning*, Victor Frankl, a well-known Viennese psychiatrist, writes, "Our search for meaning and purpose is a primary force in life. The power of this force is felt in the person who is void of meaning and purpose. The symptoms run the gamut from 'eat, drink and be merry' to the deep desire to end it all now."

1. When has life seemed meaningless for you?

2. Read 1 Peter 1:1-16. How does Peter address the recipients of his letter (vv. 1-2)?

How does this salutation address the subject of their meaning and purpose in life?

3. Consider a time when you have known someone who has lost a sense of purpose in his or her life. What did you observe about this person?

4. Look at verses 3-9 more carefully. What do these verses say about the meaning and purpose of salvation (new life)?

suffering?

faith?

5. How do verses 10-12 emphasize the importance of our meaning and purpose in life?

6. How does this passage thus far speak to your personal need for meaning in life?

7. According to verses 13-16, what is involved in holy living?

8. How can an awareness of our meaning and purpose in life affect our ability and desire to live a holy life?

9. Read 1 Peter 1:22-25. In verse 22 Peter states that the readers have purified themselves by obeying the truth. One of the results of this obedience is sincere love for their brethren. Why then does he exhort them to "love one another deeply from the heart"?

10. How is the endurance of our meaning and purpose in life further communicated in verses 23-25?

11. Think about how you spend your waking hours. How is the real purpose of your life demonstrated in your behavior?

What areas do you need to work on?

12. When caring for others who lack meaning and purpose in life, what do we have to offer them from this passage?

Pray that Christ will strengthen your understanding of his purpose in your life and help you to communicate the true meaning of life to others.

5/The Need to Be Loved and to Belong
1 John 4:7-21

I n order for infants to thrive they need to be carried, caressed and cuddled. Without this kind of touch they will die. For a child, being loved is not a luxury; it is a necessity.

This need does not cease to exist when a child becomes an adult. It may in fact intensify—depending on how adequately this need has been met throughout life. The loss or absence of human relationship as a primary source of love can contribute to depression or even a desire for death. How we are loved directly affects how we love others, receive God's love—and how we love him.

But God does not expect us to fuel our emotions and somehow manufacture love for him. Instead, God treats us the same way a responsible human father treats his own baby. God loves us first. The aging apostle John wrote of God's gift of love.

1. Think about someone who loves you. How is this love communicated to you?

How does it make you feel?

_____

2. Read 1 John 4:7-21. Find as many phrases as you can in the text that would complete this sentence, "We love because. . . ."

_____

3. What are the qualities of God's love?

_____

4. How is God's love demonstrated?

_____

5. How are you affected when you experience God's love?

_____

6. When do you have difficulty accepting God's love?

the love of others?

7. How does living in God's love affect our view of the future (vv. 16-18)? Why?

8. How do you respond to the thought in verse 18: "There is no fear in love."

9. When have you seen a person's relationship with God begin in fear, but grow to trust and eventually to love?

Why might a person's relationship with God begin partly with fear?

10. What information do you find in verses 19-21 that shows how important it is to God that we love one another?

11. When you love you become vulnerable. What enables you to risk having your love rejected?

12. How is your sense of belonging affected when someone loves you?

13. Bring to mind someone who needs to experience God's love. How might you express God's love to that person? (Be specific.)

Thank God that you are loved by him and by others, and ask him to help you to better love others.

6/The Need for Assurance
Romans 8:18-39

I f you want to receive Jesus as your Savior and become a Christian, please walk to the front of the church as we sing the final hymn," said the pastor.

Mary walked forward and stood, head bowed.

The next Sunday, the pastor gave the same invitation.

Mary walked to the front again.

The pastor raised his eyebrows, then came over and talked quietly to her. "Mary, you don't need to come to the front again. Jesus has already taken you into his family."

The next week, the pastor did not give an invitation at the end of the service. Mary came forward anyway.

Mary was a troubled young woman who had never felt assured that she was accepted anywhere. Family, friends, coworkers all regarded her as a little odd and gave her a wide berth. How could she feel assured that Jesus Christ accepted her instantly—and permanently?

Over a period of months, a sensitive pastor took time to counsel Mary. Slowly she began to believe, really believe, that God loved her and would never never leave her alone.

The apostle Paul must have known a few Marys in his lifetime. In Romans 8, he wrote for them—and for us.

1. When have you, like Mary, questioned your relationship with God?

2. Read Romans 8:18-30. How do you respond to what is stated in verse 18?

3. We do not always *feel* assured as followers of Christ. How do verses 19-25 help explain this?

4. In our culture of instant comfort and gratification, waiting for anything is not very acceptable. What do you think is involved in waiting patiently for our redemption?

5. How can eager expectation of what is to come help us cope with our present problems and sufferings?

6. What other help is offered to us during our painful wait (vv. 26-30)?

7. What is God's purpose for us (vv. 29-30)?

8. Read Romans 8:31-39. What is your emotional response to this message? Explain.

9. How do you think you would view your relationship with God in times of trouble, hardship, persecution, famine, nakedness, danger or the sword?

10. Based on the truths in this passage what should our response be to difficulties?

11. When have you been comforted and strengthened in a time of trouble because you knew God loved you and was in control?

12. What are ways that you can care for someone who needs assurance concerning his or her relationship with God?

Ask God to give you strength in times of difficulty so that you can be a witness of his power to others.

7/The Need to Persevere
James 1:2-18

I n order for athletes to get their best possible performance, they have to persevere through grueling training. Without it there is no improvement. In this passage, James suggests that the same perseverance is essential for Christians. Perseverance is not easy, however. And we live in a day of quick fixes. Except in sports, perseverance is almost an unknown.

1. When do you most feel like giving up in your Christian life?

2. Read James 1:2-18. As you look through this passage what connections do you see between perseverance and spiritual growth?

14. How can you encourage someone who is suffering to grow spiritually through perseverance?

Thank God for this source of joy and hope in the midst of trial. Ask him to help you to be an encouragement to others.

8/Caring for Those Who Doubt
Luke 7:18-30

One of the characteristics of my church that I cherish most is its respect for doubts. People there not only tolerate doubts, but they embrace the doubters, take them seriously, and care deeply for them. In this environment of acceptance and love, the doubter is freed to change and grow.

I remember Bob who challenged our prayer/fellowship class. We had prayed earnestly for the son of a class member who had gone though open-heart surgery. We were celebrating his near-miraculous healing. But Bob interrupted, "What am I supposed to think of God?" he asked. "Two years ago, we prayed for my son. But he died." The group listened, wept with him, prayed for him. But we did not try to give him answers. Not then.

---

1. How do you usually feel about yourself when you experience doubts about God?

---

2. Read Luke 7:18-30. In Matthew 11:2-14 we are told that John sent this question to Jesus from prison, and that he was soon beheaded. As Christ's fame and popularity grew (Lk 7:16-17) how *might* John the Baptist have felt as he sat in his jail cell?

3. What types of circumstances usually cause you to doubt who Jesus is or your relationship with him?

4. How did John the Baptist deal with his doubts about Jesus (vv. 18-19)?

5. How do you usually deal with your doubts?

How would you like to become more like John in dealing with them?

6. How did Jesus respond to John's doubts (vv. 22-23)?

7. Describe Christ's esteem for John in spite of John's doubts about Jesus (vv. 24-29).

8. How do you usually respond to doubt in others?

9. What have you learned from Christ's response to John about how you can care for others who are going through doubt?

10. How were all the people affected by the ministry of John the Baptist (v. 29)?

How were the Pharisees affected (v. 30)?

11. John experienced doubts. The Pharisees rebelled. What would you say is the difference between doubt and rebellion?

12. What could you do, or not do, that might encourage your doubts or those of others to lead to rebellion?

13. How could you deal with doubt in a way that allows it to deepen your faith—or the faith of others?

Ask God to help you express your doubts and deal with them in a healthy way.

9/Caring for Those in Spiritual Warfare
Ephesians 6:10-20

I n a warfare of bullets, careful aim and heavy armor win battles. In a warfare of words, eloquent speech and sharp pens overcome the opposition. But if the fight is outside the realm of sight, sound and touch, how are victories won? And how do we care for each other in the midst of such spiritual warfare?

1. How do you respond to the idea that there are spiritual forces in the universe working against God's will?

2. Read Ephesians 6:10-20. Why, according to Paul, does a believer need the whole armor of God (vv. 10-12)?

From Paul's description, what can we know about the enemy?

---

3. What kinds of spiritual opposition do you face?

---

4. Four times in verses 11-14 Paul urges his readers to *stand firm* in the battle against the devil's stratagems. What kinds of spiritual instability are we Christians susceptible to?

---

5. Think about each piece of armor that Paul calls for. What physical function does each perform?

---

6. How does its spiritual counterpart perform a similar function?

---

7. How can God's armor equip you to face the opposition described in verses 11 and 12?

8. Which piece do you need most to fight your personal spiritual battles? Explain.

9. In verses 10-12 Paul identifies our ally and enemies in warfare. In verses 13-17 he considers our preparation and tactics. Now in verses 18-20, how is the battle itself fought? Explain your answer.

10. What main obstacle do you face in more effectively fighting your spiritual battles with prayer?

How might you overcome this obstacle?

11. In our materialistic society, how can you become more sensitive to spiritual opposition and warfare?

12. Paul concludes by asking the Ephesians to pray for him. Prayer is spiritual warfare. It is also caring for each other in spiritual battle. If you do not already have people who are committed to pray for you regularly, whom could you ask?

Who can you pray for regularly?

Who could be your prayer partner?

What group might you pray with?

Begin by committing these things to prayer right now.

Leader's Notes

Leading a Bible discussion can be an enjoyable and rewarding experience. But it can also be intimidating—especially if you've never done it before. If this is how you feel, you're in good company.

When God asked Moses to lead the Israelites out of Egypt, he replied, "O Lord, please send someone else to do it!" (Ex 4:13). But God's response to all of his servants—including you—is essentially the same: "My grace is sufficient for you" (2 Cor 12:9).

There is another reason you should feel encouraged. Leading a Bible discussion is not difficult if you follow certain guidelines. You don't need to be an expert on the Bible or a trained teacher. The suggestions listed below should enable you to effectively and enjoyably fulfill your role as leader.

Using Caring People Bible Studies

Where should you begin? A good starting place is *Handbook for Caring People.* This short book helps develop some basic caring skills like listening to and communicating to people who are in pain. Additionally, it will help you understand the stages that people in grief go through and how to help people who are suffering. Most of all, this book shows how to rely on God for the strength you need to care for others. At the end of each chapter, you'll find questions for individual or group use.

For the next step you might choose *Resources for Caring People* or *The*

Character of Caring People. Resources for Caring People will show how God empowers us to serve others through Scripture, prayer, the Holy Spirit and many other gifts. *The Character of Caring People* shows what the heart of the Christian caregiver is like. The concerns which emerge within the group during the studies will provide you with guidance for what to do next. All of the guides give help and encouragement to those who want to care for others, but different groups may find some guides more useful than others.

You might want to focus on specific concerns like *Caring for People in Grief* or *Caring for People in Conflict*. Or your group might choose to study topics which reflect areas they need to grow in. For instance, those who have sick friends or relatives or who simply want to be more sensitive to the physical needs that are all around us will find *Caring for Physical Needs* helpful. Others may want to know more about the spiritual concerns people have. *Caring for Spiritual Needs* is a great resource for this. For a biblical perspective on how God wants us to deal with emotional problems, you might choose *Caring for Emotional Needs*. The key is to remember that we all have these needs. Our physical condition affects us spiritually and emotionally. A spiritual problem can have physical and emotional consequences. By covering several of these guides in sequence, members of your group will develop a complete picture of what it means to be a caring Christian.

Preparing for the Study

1. Ask God to help you understand and apply the passage in your own life. Unless this happens, you will not be prepared to lead others. Pray too for the various members of the group. Ask God to open your hearts to the message of his Word and to motivate you to action.

2. Read the introduction to the entire guide to get an overview of the subject at hand and the issues which will be explored.

3. As you begin each study, read and reread the assigned Bible passage to familiarize yourself with it.

4. This study guide is based on the New International Version of the Bible. It will help you and the group if you use this translation as the basis for your study and discussion.

5. Carefully work through each question in the study. Spend time in med-

itation and reflection as you consider how to respond.

6. Write your thoughts and responses in the space provided in the study guide. This will help you to express your understanding of the passage clearly.

7. It might help you to have a Bible dictionary handy. Use it to look up any unfamiliar words, names or places. (For additional help on how to study a passage, see chapter five of *Leading Bible Discussions,* IVP.)

8. Take the response portion of each study seriously. Consider what this means for your life—what changes you might need to make in your lifestyle and/or actions you need to take in the world. Remember that the group will follow your lead in responding to the studies.

Leading the Study

1. Begin the study on time. Open with prayer, asking God to help the group to understand and apply the passage.

2. Be sure that everyone in your group has a study guide. Encourage the group to prepare beforehand for each discussion by reading the introduction to the guide and by working through the questions in the study.

3. At the beginning of your first time together, explain that these studies are meant to be discussions, not lectures. Encourage the members of the group to participate. However, do not put pressure on those who may be hesitant to speak during the first few sessions.

4. Have a group member read the introductory paragraph at the beginning of the discussion. This will orient the group to the topic of the study.

5. Every study begins with an "approach" question, which is meant to be asked before the passage is read. These questions are important for several reasons.

First, there is always a stiffness that needs to be overcome before people will begin to talk openly. A good question will break the ice.

Second, most people will have lots of different things going on in their minds (dinner, an important meeting coming up, how to get the car fixed) that will have nothing to do with the study. A creative question will get their attention and draw them into the discussion.

Third, approach questions can reveal where our thoughts or feelings need to be transformed by Scripture. That is why it is especially important not to read the passage before the approach question is asked. The passage will tend to color the honest reactions people would otherwise give because they are, of course, supposed to think the way the Bible does.

6. Have a group member read aloud the passage to be studied.

7. As you ask the questions, keep in mind that they are designed to be used just as they are written. You may simply read them aloud. Or you may prefer to express them in your own words. There may be times when it is appropriate to deviate from the study guide. For example, a question may have already been answered. If so, move on to the next question. Or someone may raise an important question not covered in the guide. Take time to discuss it, but try to keep the group from going off on tangents.

8. Avoid answering your own questions. If necessary, repeat or rephrase them until they are clearly understood. An eager group quickly becomes passive and silent if they think the leader will do most of the talking.

9. Don't be afraid of silence. People may need time to think about the question before formulating their answers.

10. Don't be content with just one answer. Ask, "What do the rest of you think?" or "Anything else?" until several people have given answers to the question.

11. Acknowledge all contributions. Try to be affirming whenever possible. Never reject an answer. If it is clearly off-base, ask, "Which verse led you to that conclusion?" or again, "What do the rest of you think?"

12. Don't expect every answer to be addressed to you, even though this will probably happen at first. As group members become more at ease, they will begin to truly interact with each other. This is one sign of healthy discussion.

13. Don't be afraid of controversy. It can be very stimulating. If you don't resolve an issue completely, don't be frustrated. Move on and keep it in mind for later. A subsequent study may solve the problem.

14. Periodically summarize what the group has said about the passage. This helps to draw together the various ideas mentioned and gives continuity to the study. But don't preach.

15. Don't skip over the response questions. It's important that we not lose the focus of helping others even as we reflect on ourselves. Be willing to get things started by describing how you have been affected by the study.

16. Conclude your time together with conversational prayer. Ask for God's help in following through on the commitments you've made.

17. End on time. Many more suggestions and helps are found in *Small Group Leader's Handbook* and *Good Things Come in Small Groups* (both from IVP). Reading through one of these books would be worth your time.

Listening to Emotional Pain

Caring People Bible Studies are designed to take seriously the pain and struggle that is part of life. People will experience a variety of emotions during these studies. Keep in mind that you are not expected to act as a professional counselor. However, part of your role as group leader may be to listen to emotional pain. Listening is a gift which you can give to a person who is hurting. For many people, it is not an easy gift to give. The following suggestions will help you to listen more effectively to people in emotional pain.

1. Remember that you are not responsible to take the pain away. People in helping relationships often feel that they are being asked to make the other person feel better. This may be related to the helper not being comfortable with painful feelings.

2. Not only are you not responsible to take the pain away, one of the things people need most is an opportunity to face and to experience the pain in their lives. Many have spent years denying their pain and running from it. Healing can come when we are able to face our pain in the presence of someone who cares about us. Rather than trying to take the pain away, then, commit yourself to listening attentively as it is expressed.

3. Realize that some group members may not feel comfortable with others' expressions of sadness or anger. You may want to acknowledge that such emotions are uncomfortable, but say that learning to feel our own pain is often the first step in helping others with their pain.

4. Be very cautious about giving answers and advice. Advice and answers may make you feel better or feel competent, but they may also minimize people's problems and their painful feelings. Simple solutions rarely work, and they can easily communicate "You should be better now" or "You shouldn't really be talking about this."

5. Be sure to communicate direct affirmation any time people talk about their painful emotions. It takes courage to talk about our pain because it creates anxiety for us. It is a great gift to be trusted by those who are struggling.

The following notes refer to specific questions in the study:

Study 1. What Are Spiritual Needs? Psalm 38.

Purpose: To consider the far-reaching effects of spiritual needs.

Questions 2-4. The psalmist seems to be saying that he is suffering because God's hand of judgment is upon him. Sin is the cause of all his distress, for example, "my sin" (v. 3), "My guilt has overwhelmed me" (v. 4), "my sinful folly" (v. 5).

Beginning with festering wounds, the consequences of his sinful folly are graphically described: a pain-racked body, bent and bowed like that of a mourner; his whole frame fevered and diseased. The description then gradually turns from outward symptoms of the flesh to evidences of an inner malady which is well known to God. There is a general sense of numbness and incapacity, the inarticulate groaning of an aching heart and a troubled conscience. Such a moral malady finds expression in a throbbing heart, a loss of zest in life, dullness of vision, and a suspicion on the part of friends and even of kinsmen which causes them to hold aloof from him, as if he were a leper. (*The New Bible Commentary*, rev. [Grand Rapids: Eerdmans, 1973], p. 475.)

Note: Bible scholars disagree about whether Psalm 38 is a prayer for the sick or a prayer for the penitent sinner. It might be either, or both. In David's time, as in ours, the symptoms intertwined. Be careful, however, as your group works through this study that people do not assume that all physical suffering has a spiritual cause. To do so may bring unnecessary pain to people who are physically ill—but still walking closely with their Lord. Jesus spoke against such assumptions in John 9:1-3.

Question 6. Your group may be hesitant to speak of such a painful and personal event. Be ready with a relatively casual experience from your own life.

Question 7. Help the group to be specific and thorough in response to this question because there are people all around us with these kinds of needs.

Question 8. He admits his sin, and recognizes that it is this which is the root cause of his sorrow and care.

Question 9. One of the considerations in responding to this question is how confident are we that God will answer?

"The prayer concludes with an urgent call to the Lord not to forsake him nor to be slow to intervene. Faith has not yet risen to triumphant certainty yet, but it is implicit in the final words, *O Lord, my salvation*" (*The New Bible Commentary*, p. 475).

Study 2. Recognizing Spiritual Needs. Matthew 9:1-13.

Purpose: To consider Christ's ability to recognize spiritual need and his authority to meet those needs. To grow in our own sensitivity to spiritual needs.

Question 1. Part of this discussion may revolve around the question "What is a spiritual need?" That is fine. There is help in the introduction to this guide on what a spiritual need is.

Question 3. First and foremost Christ's actions were a demonstration of his astute awareness of the needs of individuals. He saw what others did not see. He not only recognized the need, but also demonstrated the authority and ability to meet that need.

Even if the paralytic had not been healed physically, having his sins forgiven and being in a right relationship with God was the greatest thing that could have happened to him—far beyond his or his friends' expectations.

Second, Christ's words demonstrate that we are spiritual and emotional as well as physical beings.

Third, Jesus was demonstrating his authority to the religious leaders as well as to the crowd. He recognized their spiritual needs too.

And finally, this was an occasion for Jesus to work out his agenda, that of "calling sinners to repentance." Every person is in spiritual need, and Jesus recognized this fact.

Question 4. As we consider caring for others who are in spiritual need, it is significant that the faith of friends played such an important role in this process. The faith may have included that of the patient as well as his friends. There is great power in corporate faith.

Question 5. Prayer for others is certainly one important way our faith affects how we care for others. We can bring their needs to Jesus who can help them.

Question 6. The crowd seemed to have some understanding of the implications of who Jesus was. The religious leaders, however, correctly understood his claim to deity—and assumed it was impossible. If Jesus had been merely a man, as the crowd assumed in verse 8, the accusation of blasphemy would have been entirely correct.

Question 8. The basic concern of both was to criticize and "catch" Jesus rather than to get to know him and be changed by him. Their whole religious system and their authority in it was being threatened by this person.

"It was easier to speak of forgiveness because it could not be tested. Yet the actual provision of forgiveness required a greater authority even than of healing a paralyzed man. As in the previous story something physical was a sign of psychological cure, so here something physical is a sign of a spiritual cure" (*The New Bible Commentary*, p. 827).

Question 10. Jesus is the "physician." "The sick" are sinners who recognize their need for God's forgiveness. "The healthy" would be anyone without sin. In reality, there were not any healthy people in this passage. But since the Pharisees and the teachers of the Law felt no spiritual need for Jesus, he, perhaps with a hint of sarcasm, called them "healthy."

Question 12. Spiritual needs are all around us. Everyone has them. We need, as Jesus did, to look beyond the surface. Jesus looked straight into the heart. We humans cannot do that. But we can be aware that physical and spiritual needs often coexist. And we can encourage the people we serve to look within their own hearts.

Study 3. The Need for a Relationship with God. Romans 5:1-11.

Purpose: To understand that a right relationship with God is the very foundation of having our spiritual needs satisfied.

Question 2. This question serves as an overview of the passage. Use it to lead the group in scanning the passage for nearly a dozen answers. Later questions will look more in-depth at these benefits.

Question 4. "Paul is stating that as believers we now stand in a place of highest privilege. Not only has God declared us not guilty; he has drawn us close to him. Instead of enemies, we have become his friends—in fact, his own children" (*Life Application Bible* [Wheaton, Ill.: Tyndale, 1986], p. 1708).

Help the group to grapple with what grace is all about. What does this grace mean in our lives on a day-by-day basis? Discuss the process of becoming more and more like Jesus.

Paul never contemplates the possibility of a justification which was not invariably followed by a sanctification: justification and sanctification are for him inseparably connected in fact.

The believer does not enter into favour with God on his own merit. The idea of access is introduction into the presence-chamber of the king. This presentation before the royal throne is effected by one near the monarch himself. Here it is Jesus who leads us to God. The apostle describes the active favour of the Father to believers by the term grace. The justified are ushered into a state of grace which brings security and confidence. (*The New Bible Commentary*, p. 1024.)

"The word 'grace' is preferred to mercy, because it includes the idea of the divine power which equips a man to live a moral life" (J. D. Douglas, ed., *The New Bible Dictionary* [Wheaton, Ill.: Tyndale House, 1962], p. 492).

Question 5. We are told to rejoice in the hope of the glory of God. Hope has to do with the future, with what is coming. God's glory gives us hope because we *will* share in his glory—we are becoming like him. How? Through suffering. So we rejoice in suffering because it is a part of the process of becoming like him which gives us hope. In other words, "suffering produces perseverance; perseverance produces character; and character hope. (Change in our character makes us hopeful.) And hope does not disappoint us because God has poured out his love into our hearts by the Holy Spirit, whom he has given us. (The Holy Spirit is working in us in this process.)

John Stott writes of the glory of God, "But what is the 'glory of God'? The glory of God is the manifestation of God, his radiant splendor, the outward shining of his inward being. And already his glory has been partly revealed—in the universe, in human beings and supremely in Jesus Christ. . . . One day however, the glory of God will be fully revealed, and 'we exult in hope of this prospect.' " (*Believing and Obeying Jesus Christ* (Downers Grove, Ill.: InterVarsity Press, 1980], p. 95.)

Question 5. Do not be afraid of silence. Allow the group to think. It is especially needed in application questions. Some application questions take more time than others. It always helps to set the pace when the leader is prepared to share from his or her own experience.

Encourage the group members to explore how their attitudes toward suffering can become more biblical. "We are to rejoice in suffering—not because we are masochists who enjoy pain, but because God uses suffering to transform our character" (Jack Kuhatschek, *Romans: Becoming New in Christ* [Downers Grove, Ill.: InterVarsity Press, 1986], p. 83).

Question 8. *The New Bible Commentary* provides this helpful summary:

Paul continues his assertion of the security of the believer's righteousness with a triumphant *a fortiori* argument. The *love* of God toward us as undeserving and rebellious sinners is testified by the sacrifice of His Son on our behalf, a death upon the cross which brings us into a completely new relation with Him. This amazing love of God in putting us right with Himself is the greatest fact of our salvation. God achieved reconciliation by the death of his Son when we were in a state of unbelieving hostility. Much more, then shall God be able to keep us in peace with Himself as His friends by the risen life of His Son. If God can accomplish our justification, beyond doubt He can also accomplish our sanctification. The idea is all of life, the believer's life through the Saviour's life. Paul does not use the term "sanctification" in his measuring of the greater and the great. His contrast is between justification and salvation. But the latter term has just this meaning of progressive holiness. In union with Christ as a living Lord we are empowered to live the holy life of moral and spiritual overcoming so that we, in our sanctified personality, escape the wrath of God on the judgment day through the completed and efficacious work of Jesus Christ. (p. 1025)

Study 4. The Need for Meaning and Purpose. 1 Peter 1:1-16, 22-25.

Purpose: To understand that meaning and purpose in life is a basic spiritual need and that only the gospel satisfies that need.

Question 2. This salutation gives a clear statement of meaning and purpose. It tells them that they are elect, the chosen of God *for* obedience to Jesus

Christ. It also speaks of their circumstances. The rest of this passage explains how this greeting is fleshed out.

Question 3. Help the group to look beyond the superficial aspects of this question. Discussing the symptoms seen in others should help members to increase their awareness of this spiritual need in others as well as in themselves.

Question 4. This paragraph needs to be carefully dissected in order to respond adequately to this question. It is cause for careful preparation by the leader ahead of time. List all that has to do with salvation, with faith and with suffering. Some thoughts overlap.

In verse 9 *your souls* might be better translated "yourselves."

Question 9. Sincere love for each other is an inward change that has been produced in the believer through their purification. Peter is exhorting believers to milk love for all it is worth—actively, deeply put it into practice, flesh it out, care for each other in practical ways. Nurture and practice what has already been produced in them.

"The life of obedience already referred to (vv. 2, 14) will result in the purity required before God of those who are to reflect the Father's holiness, and should lead to a genuine love for one's fellow-Christians: the reality of this should be evidenced by its intensity (earnestly) and depth (from the heart)" (*The New Bible Commentary*, p. 1240).

Question 11. Be careful not to get caught up in dichotomizing life by saying, for instance, "Work is secular, and prayer is sacred." Rather, be concerned with attitudes, motivation and what it is to offer all of life, all of who we are and all of what we do, for God's glory.

Study 5. The Need to Be Loved and to Belong. 1 John 4:7-21.

Purpose: To consider the significance of God's love for us individually; to grow in demonstrating God's love to others.

Questions 2-4. Lead the group through the whole passage for these answers. For questions 3 and 4, do not be content with members listing one-word answers. Go on to consider the meaning behind the words.

Questions 5-6. Encourage open discussion about how much we need and are affected by the love of God. Talk sensitively and openly about the difficulties that we have in receiving his love.

Question 8. This is a time when truth and experience can seem to be far apart. Help the group to examine where there is fear in their relationship with God and with others in spite of being loved by God and others.

Question 13. Help the group to think about how God expresses his love to us. We represent him to others and can express love in the same ways, that is, through listening, walking through pain with them, accepting people where they are, communicating hope, and communicating their value.

Study 6. The Need for Assurance. Romans 8:18-39.

Purpose: To understand more fully the assurance that we have as Christians.

Question 3. Larry Crabb, a Christian psychologist, in his book *Inside Out* talks about longings that we have. He says that there are certain longings that will not be satisfied this side of heaven. We do not like living with unsatisfied longings. We try to take shortcuts to satisfy them instead of feeling and living with them. These verses explain some of this when they speak of the whole creation groaning, and of Christians groaning inwardly as we wait eagerly.

"Some Christians believe the normal Christian life is meant to be free from sickness, suffering and difficulty. They claim that if we are not healthy, wealthy and happy it is because of personal sin or disbelief. This passage provides a powerful corrective to this kind of thinking" (Kuhatschek, *Romans,* p. 87).

We have assurance not because our lives are free from suffering, but because we triumph in spite of our suffering.

Question 4. One aspect of "patiently waiting" is accepting the pain of longings, groanings that are not satisfied on earth—that will be satisfied only when we are completely redeemed. It is accepting the pain. It is letting the pain serve as a reminder that this is not the end, that can move us on to eager expectation.

"Waiting, in the Christian sense, is both an active and a passive experience. Our waiting is to be characterized by a strong sense of anticipation.

"But while we wait in anticipation we are not demanding or angry with God for not coming according to our timetable. We wait in patient humility for the time when he is ready to complete his work" (Steve Eyre, *Christian Beliefs* [Downers Grove, Ill.: InterVarsity Press, 1989], p. 60).

Question 6. Wonderful help is offered. Help the group to examine these verses thoroughly.

Question 7. "In order to understand this verse we must understand Paul's definition of good. Obviously from the context it cannot mean freedom from suffering, hardship or difficulty. His good purpose is that we become conformed to the image of his son" (Kuhatschek, *Romans*, p. 88).

Question 8. In order to capture the emotional impact of Paul's words, ask an expressive reader to read this entire passage aloud. Do not read by verses or paragraphs.

Question 9. Even though each person should respond to only one of the difficult circumstances Paul mentions, allow enough different people to respond so that the group addresses most of the problems.

Study 7. The Need to Persevere. James 1:2-18.

Purpose: To consider the need for perseverance and to see this as a basic spiritual need.

Question 2. This is an overview question because you need to look through the whole passage for the answers. It also focuses on the topic of perseverance as a spiritual need.

Help the group to discover the spiritual benefits that rely on perseverance. Some of these are: reaching maturity, completion (v. 4), receiving wisdom from God (v. 6), believing and not doubting, receiving the crown of life (v. 12), and resisting temptation (vv. 13-15). Spiritual disaster can occur when we do not persevere.

Confusion could arise about what perseverance is all about. You may want to make sure the group's understanding of perseverance is adequate. James is not talking about stubbornness or grinning and bearing it. He speaks of being steadfast in purpose, of persisting in a right direction, of doing the right thing in spite of difficulty.

Question 8. This may elicit questions about the place of doubt in the Christian life. While a period of questioning can be a healthy time that leads to growth, a life characterized by indecisiveness is worthless in God's sight. James draws two extremes to make his point.

Question 9. Wealth, power and status mean nothing to God. The poor should acknowledge this, rejoice and persevere. Some people who are rich have a tendency to rely on their riches for a sense of purpose and reason for living. They need to realize that these things mean nothing to God. In fact they will pass away. For those who overvalue riches, it often takes a crisis for them to turn to God. This is good when it happens. But when the poor have something good happen they may be less likely to give themselves the credit. The poor know it had to come from God, and so they turn to him in thanks. Each situation increases reliance on God. Reliance on God increases perseverance.

Question 13. Note on "firstfruits": The first fruits of the harvest were specifically committed to God as part of the regular thanksgiving of each Israelite (see Lev 23:9-11). The term is often used as a metaphor to signify priority of position and importance in God's sight (for example, see Jer 2:3 RSV).

Study 8. Caring for Those Who Doubt. Luke 7:18-30.

Purpose: To know the response that we can expect from Jesus when we doubt, and to discuss how we can care for others who doubt.

Question 2. Though this is a speculative question I believe it will help to identify with John and thereby to look at our own doubts.

Question 3. Considering this question helps us to look at the types of doubts we have and to see possible patterns or predictable warning signs to watch for in ourselves.

Question 4. This is an important question. It is not wrong to doubt. How we choose to deal with our doubts is what is important. Help the group not to pass over this issue in a shallow way.

John was direct in his doubts. He acknowledges them. In fact, he went straight to Jesus with them. Not only was he honest with himself, he allowed himself to hear from Jesus, so that he could believe the truth that Jesus spoke.

John could have denied his doubts to himself and to others. He could have pretended that they did not exist. He could have put up the Christian front or put on a mask. If he had done so, he would have missed great truth and encouragement from the Lord Jesus.

Finally, others ("all the people," v. 29) would have missed an opportunity for truth and growth if John had covered his doubt.

Question 5. Lead the group members in honestly looking at how they deal with their doubts and to consider whether or not they need to change.

Question 6. What did Jesus mean by the words "fall away on account of me" (v. 23)? This is probably a gentle rebuke to his cousin John—more like encouragement than criticism. A more likely translation comes from the Jerusalem Bible: "Happy is the man who does not lose faith in me."

Question 7. It is important that Jesus not only accepted and responded to John's doubts but that his esteem for John was not lessened.

What did Jesus mean when he said of John, "Yet the one who is least in the kingdom of God is greater than he" (v. 28)? Bible scholar William Hendriksen answers this way:

> This cannot mean that John, after all, was not a saved man. Perish the very thought! . . . The one least in the kingdom was greater than John in the sense that he was more highly privileged, for the Baptist in his prison was not in such close touch with Jesus as was this one. And it was this very circumstance which had also contributed to the herald's confusion with respect to whether or not Jesus was truly the Messiah. (William Hendriksen, *The Gospel of Luke* [Grand Rapids, Mich.: Baker, 1978], p. 398.)

Question 8. Often we do not accept, respond to correctly, or hold in high esteem, people who are struggling with doubt.

Question 11. Both rebellion and doubt are spiritual needs. There is a difference in the two. John the Baptist demonstrates doubt. The religious leaders in this passage demonstrate rebellion. Possibly the core of the issue is choice and attitude.

The Pharisees and experts in the Law *rejected* God's purpose for themselves. John, on the other hand, went toward God, not away from him. He desired resolution, restored relationship, truth. His attitude was that of openness and desire for change.

Study 9. Caring for Those in Spiritual Warfare. Ephesians 6:10-20.

Purpose: To become more astute in recognizing and preparing for spiritual warfare; to consider how we can care for each other in the midst of spiritual warfare.

Question 1. There may be some in your group who do not believe in a personal devil. Allow them to express their views without getting into a big discussion of whether or not they are right. As the study moves on, Paul's position should become plain.

Question 3. As you prepare for leading this study think carefully about spiritual opposition that you face. Share it with the group. Set the stage for group members to *begin* to look at the spiritual world. It is a foreign concept to some people. To others it is merely a theoretical, theological concept to which they give mental assent. Still others have begun to recognize it in their own experiences. In your discussion, people should grow beyond where they are in their awareness.

Question 5. Get an overview as you consider each piece of armor. Keep the time limit in mind as you move through this question. It is most important to get the general idea of how we are prepared.

About the Author

Phyllis J. Le Peau is a registered nurse and a former Nurses Christian Fellowship staffworker. Currently, she is assistant program director for Wellness, Inc. Phyllis is also the author of the Fruit of the Spirit Bible Studies Kindness, Gentleness and Joy (Zondervan) and coauthor of Disciplemakers' Handbook (IVP). With her husband, Andy, she has coauthored One Plus One Equals One and the LifeGuide® Bible Studies Ephesians and James (IVP/SU). She and her husband live in Downers Grove, Illinois, with their four children.

Caring People Bible Studies from InterVarsity Press
By Phyllis J. Le Peau

Handbook for Caring People (coauthored by Bonnie J. Miller). This book provides simple, time-tested principles for dealing with the pain, the questions and the crises people face. You will get the basic tools for communication plus some practical suggestions. Questions for group discussion are at the end of each chapter.

Resources for Caring People. Through God, we have the resources we need to help others. God has given us Scripture, prayer, the Holy Spirit, listening and acceptance. This guide will show you how he works through people like you every day. 8 studies.

The Character of Caring People. The key to caring is character. These Bible studies will show you how to focus on the gifts of caring which God has given you—such as hospitality, generosity and encouragement. 8 studies.

Caring for Spiritual Needs. A relationship with God. Meaning and purpose. Belonging. Love. Assurance. These are just some of the spiritual needs that we all have. This Bible study guide will help you learn how these needs can be met in your life and in the lives of others. 9 studies.

Caring for Emotional Needs. We think we have to act like we have it all together, yet sometimes we are lonely, afraid or depressed. Christians have emotional needs just like everyone else. This Bible study guide shows how to find emotional health for ourselves and how to help others. 9 studies.

Caring for Physical Needs. When we are sick or when our basic needs for food, clothing and adequate housing are not being met, our whole being—body, spirit and emotion—is affected. When we care for the physical needs of others, we are showing God's love. These Bible studies will help you learn to do that. 8 studies.

Caring for People in Conflict. Divided churches. Broken friendships. Angry children. Torn marriages. We all have to deal with conflict and the emotions which accompany it. These studies will show you how God can bring healing and reconciliation. 9 studies.

Caring for People in Grief. Because sin brought death into the world, we all have to look into death's ugly face at one time or another. These Bible studies cover the issues which consume those who are grieving—fear, peace, grace and hope—and show you how to provide them with comfort. 9 studies.